PEARL HARBOR

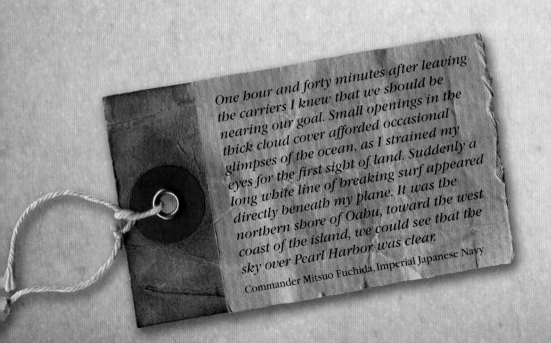

One hour and forty minutes after leaving the carriers I knew that we should be nearing our goal. Small openings in the thick cloud cover afforded occasional glimpses of the ocean, as I strained my eyes for the first sight of land. Suddenly a long white line of breaking surf appeared directly beneath my plane. It was the northern shore of Oahu, toward the west coast of the island, we could see that the sky over Pearl Harbor was clear.

Commander Mitsuo Fuchida, Imperial Japanese Navy

A PLACE IN HISTORY

PEARL HARBOR

**STEWART ROSS AND
JOE WOODWARD**

ARCTURUS

This edition first published in 2010 by Arcturus Publishing
Distributed by Black Rabbit Books
P.O. Box 3263
Mankato
Minnesota MN 56002

Printed in China

Series concept: Alex Woolf
Editors: Sean Connolly and Alex Woolf
Designer: Phipps Design
Picture research: Alex Woolf
Map illustrators: Stefan Chabluk and
The Map Studio

Library of Congress Cataloging-in-Publication Data

Ross, Stewart.
  Pearl Harbor / Stewart Ross and Joe Woodward.
    p. cm. -- (A place in history)
  Includes bibliographical references and index.
  ISBN 978-1-84837-676-2 (library binding)
 1. Pearl Harbor (Hawaii), Attack on, 1941--Juvenile literature.
2. World War, 1939-1945--Causes--Juvenile literature. 3.
Japan--Foreign relations--United States--Juvenile literature. 4.
United States--Foreign relations--Japan--Juvenile literature. I.
Woodward, Joe. II. Title.
  D767.92.R68 2011
  940.54'26693--dc22
              2010017108

Picture credits:
Arcturus: 9 (Stefan Chabluk), 27 (The Map Studio), 29 (The Map Studio).
Corbis: cover *both* (Bettmann), 6–7 (Bettmann), 8 (Bettmann), 10 (Bettmann),
12 (Schenectady Museum; Hall of Electrical History Foundation), 14 (Bettmann),
15, 16, 18 (Bettmann), 19 (Bettmann), 20 (Bettmann), 24 (Bettmann), 26
(Bettmann), 28 (Bettmann), 30 (Bettmann), 31 (Bettmann), 32 (Bettmann), 33
(Bettmann), 34, 36 (Bettmann), 37 (Bettmann), 38 (Bettmann), 39 (Bettmann),
40 (Reuters), 41 (Bettmann), 42 (Bettmann).
Getty Images: 11 (Time & Life Pictures), 13 (Hulton Archive), 17 (Keystone/
Hulton Archive), 21 (Popperfoto), 22 (Hulton Archive), 23 (Thomas D. McAvoy/
Time & Life Pictures), 25 (MPI/Hulton Archive).
Shutterstock: 43 (TechWizard).

Cover pictures:
Background: The battleships USS *West Virginia* and USS *Tennessee* in flames
after the Japanese surprise attack on Pearl Harbor on December 7, 1941.
Foreground: President Franklin D. Roosevelt, wearing a black armband, signs
the United States' declaration of war against Japan on December 8, 1941.

Every attempt has been made to clear copyright. Should there be any
inadvertent omission, please apply to the publisher for rectification.

SL001442US   Supplier 03 Date 0510

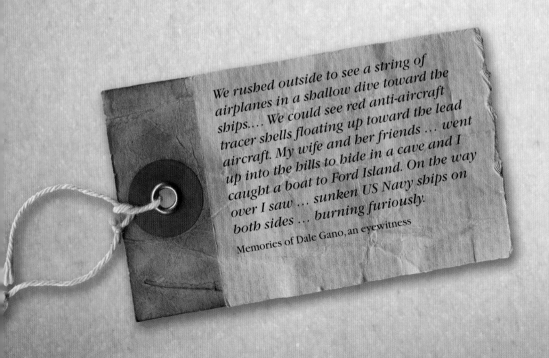

We rushed outside to see a string of airplanes in a shallow dive toward the ships.... We could see red anti-aircraft tracer shells floating up toward the lead aircraft. My wife and her friends ... went up into the hills to hide in a cave and I caught a boat to Ford Island. On the way over I saw ... sunken US Navy ships on both sides ... burning furiously.

Memories of Dale Gano, an eyewitness

CONTENTS

1.

Dawn, December 7, 1941: Japanese carrier-borne Mitsubishi dive bombers line up on deck ready for takeoff. A few hours later they were screaming into attack at Pearl Harbor.

6

Shortly after dawn on December 7, 1941, Commander Mitsuo Fuchida stepped from the flight deck of the Japanese aircraft carrier *Akagi* and into the cockpit of his Nakajima B5N bomber. Behind him, rows of torpedo bombers and fighters stood in readiness. Alongside the *Akagi* steamed six other Japanese carriers, their flight decks packed with aircraft. Beyond them, the waiting pilots could see the outlines of the escort battleships and destroyers of the naval Striking Force. Far in front, midget submarines stealthily prepared to approach their target.

The Striking Force was the most powerful aircraft carrier fleet the world had ever seen. It had been assembled for one audacious mission: a surprise air assault on the unsuspecting US Pacific Fleet at its home base in Hawaii. If the mission, known as Operation Z, was successful, then the only force capable of stopping a Japanese offensive into Southeast Asia would be destroyed before war had even been declared.

At 06:00 Commander Fuchida received the order he had been waiting for. His bomber thundered along the flight deck and into the gray skies over the Pacific. A total of 353 Japanese aircraft, dive bombers, torpedo planes, and fighters followed him, their pilots gathering in two waves over the Striking Force, before setting course for the Hawaiian Islands—their target: Pearl Harbor.

2 PEARL WATERS

Pearl Harbor is a deep, Y-shaped inlet on the southern coast of Oahu, the third largest of the Hawaiian Islands. This beautiful archipelago stretches in a 2,000-mile (3,000-kilometer) arc across the mid-Pacific. Known in the Hawaiian language as Wai Momi, meaning "Pearl Waters," the famous harbor lies some 2,385 miles (3,850 kilometers) west of San Francisco, 4,100 miles (6,500 kilometers) east of Tokyo, and 4,600 miles (7,300 kilometers) north of Australia. Such is the strategic importance of this position, it is said to stand at the "crossroads of the Pacific."

US colony

The British explorer Captain James Cook was the first European to land on the Hawaiian Islands (1778). He found them inhabited by Polynesians who had crossed there in huge seagoing canoes a thousand years before. Following Cook's visit, these peoples were soon outnumbered by immigrants, mainly from the United States.

A British expedition, led by the explorer Captain James Cook, lands on the Hawaiian Islands, 1778. As was the European custom at the time, he gave them a Western name, the "Sandwich Islands."

VOICES

Naming the islands

Besides these six [islands], which we can distinguish by their names, it appeared that the inhabitants … were acquainted with some other islands both to the eastward and westward. I named the whole group the Sandwich Islands, in honor of the Earl of Sandwich.

Captain Cook, 1778. "Hawaii" became the commonly used name in the 19th century.

The Hawaiian Island chain comprises hundreds of islands spread over across the Pacific Ocean. The main islands are shown on this map.

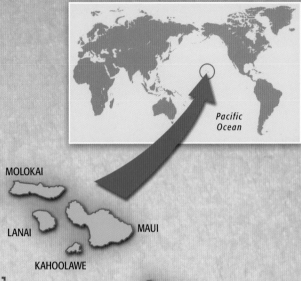

FACT FILE

Cutting the coral

The US Navy first used Honolulu as a base in 1860. Naval Station Hawaii was formally established in 1899–1900. Work began immediately on widening and deepening access to Pearl Harbor by dredging through the coral reef that lay across the port's narrow entrance. By 1903 the seaway was large enough for the first battleship, USS *Wisconsin*, to steam into Pearl Harbor.

American business, notably whaling and sugar farming, also moved in, and in 1851 King Kamehameha III of Hawaii put his country under US protection. From this point onward, Hawaiian independence was doomed.

A US–Hawaii treaty of 1875 increased US influence, and 12 years later the king was forced to accept a government dominated by white sugar farmers. The monarchy collapsed soon afterward. In 1900 the jewels of the Pacific that Mark Twain called "the loveliest fleet of islands that lies anchored in any ocean" were formally annexed to the United States as "overseas territories."

The US Navy had moved in some time before. During the 1880s, in exchange for allowing Hawaiian sugar into the United States duty-free, the navy was granted the exclusive right to use Pearl Harbor. The entrance was soon dredged to allow large warships to enter. In a flurry of construction, the next few years saw wharves, dry docks, maintenance yards, store rooms, and barracks spring up along the southern shore of the lagoon, opposite Ford Island. The army came in too, setting up an air base at Hickam Field near the harbor entrance. In 1914 it began building the large Schofield Barracks, a building that remains to this day.

Sitting ducks: lines of warships, some in pairs, are clearly visible in this aerial photograph of Pearl Harbor taken shortly before the Japanese attack.

The naval base

For almost a century after its foundation, the United States had looked east, toward Europe, for its friends, enemies, and trading partners. But by the second half of the 19th century this situation was changing. As Japan strove to become a modern, Western-style power, so the United States found its gaze turning more to the west. It was concerned over the future of China, too, and an increasing portion of its trade went to Asia via the ports on America's western seaboard. In 1898, during the Spanish-American War,

VOICES

The importance of Pearl Harbor, 1941

The Navy industrial plant is the major industrial activity in the islands and is much larger than all the civilian industrial plants combined. In a sense, the whole district is the naval base, and unlike continental [US] naval districts, it is almost wholly dependent upon sea communications to the mainland for supplies and personnel.

US Navy plan for the Pearl Harbor District, 1941

the United States became heavily involved in the Philippines and, by 1902, that island country had also become a US colony. It was against this background that the US Navy started expanding its Pearl Harbor base.

After a lull following World War I (1914–18), by the 1930s Pearl Harbor was once again under development. Between 1936 and 1940 more than $100 million was spent upgrading the port, including enlarging the entrance yet again to accommodate the latest battleships and aircraft carriers. It now had a submarine base and the number of naval personnel rose to more than 1,000. In February 1941 the US Navy made the crucial decision to divide its fleet. One half remained in the Atlantic. The other, now known as the Pacific Fleet, had its principal base and operational headquarters at Pearl Harbor.

FACT FILE

Ships and planes

On the morning of December 7, 1941, over half the US Pacific Fleet, including all its aircraft carriers, was at sea. Some 99 vessels, large and small, remained in Pearl Harbor. Among their number were eight battleships, eight cruisers, 30 destroyers, and four submarines. In addition there were 390 planes on the surrounding airfields.

Changing history

Pearl Harbor was now the very heart of US power in the Pacific, and it was against this highly prestigious site that the Japanese launched their devastating surprise attack at dawn on December 7, 1941. The unannounced strike changed the history of the world. Firstly, it brought the United States into World War II. Congress declared war on Japan the very next day, which soon led to a state of war with Germany and Italy. Secondly, the experience of the war changed the United States from an inward-looking major power to an outward-looking global superpower.

Ready for war? US soldiers parade on board a warship exercising in the Pacific, near Hawaii, in September 1940.

3. TWO RISING POWERS

The gradual breakdown in relations between Japan and the United States began after World War I. Before that, the United States had been an inspiration for Japan's process of Westernization, and the two countries had fought on the same side in 1917-18. Thereafter tensions began to mount as the two great powers found their interests in conflict, especially over China. Japan needed raw materials for its industry while its military leaders sought glory and empire. The United States wanted to maintain an "open door" to China for all nations and was hostile to the idea of empire. A clash between two such opposing attitudes was almost inevitable.

Japan turns west

Between the 1630s and the 19th century Japan declared itself a "closed country." Foreign visitors and ways were rejected out of hand. This changed in 1853-54 when Commodore Matthew Perry of the US Navy forced the Japanese government to accept US merchants into some Japanese ports. Traders from other nations followed. The huge tensions and changes resulting from this alien intrusion caused the traditional Japanese system of government to collapse.

FACT FILE

Japan's need for raw materials

Japan's exports increased eightfold between 1878 and 1900, quadrupled again by 1914, and then tripled by 1924. Many exports were goods manufactured in Japanese factories from imported raw materials. Significantly, the value of imports climbed from 86 million yen per year in 1890–94 to 2.4 billion yen per year in 1920–24: Japan's economy was becoming heavily dependent upon imports, especially iron and oil.

A new global industrial power: Japanese workers make electrical machinery in the Shibaura Engineering Works between the wars.

A dramatic painting of the sinking of the Russian battleship *Borodino* under Japanese fire at the Battle of Tsushima, May 28, 1905.

This led to a coup, known as the Meiji Restoration (1868), which brought in a modernizing government.

Under the broadminded influence of the young emperor Mutsuhito, Japan began the process of rapid Westernization and industrialization. The systems of law, education and government were all brought into line with the practices of the United States and Western Europe. Japanese students traveled the world to learn the secrets of modern banking and industry, and Western entrepreneurs helped establish new factories and mines in Japan. The Japanese responded to these changes with skill, energy, and efficiency.

The results startled the world. Between 1870 and 1913 Japan's average annual growth rate was above that of all other industrial nations apart from the United States. The country dramatically demonstrated its newfound power in 1904–05, when it fought a successful war against its gigantic neighbor Russia. The sinking of Russia's Baltic fleet in the Tsushima Straits announced the arrival of a formidable new naval power. Korea was seized as part of the spoils of war and, in 1910, became a Japanese colony.

VOICES

Looking west

We recognize the excellence of Western civilization. We value the Western theories of rights, liberty, and equality; and we respect Western philosophy and morals … Above all, we esteem Western science, economics, and industry. These, however, ought not to be adopted because they are Western; they ought to be adopted only if they can contribute to Japan's welfare.

Kuga Katsunan, a prominent Japanese journalist, 1889

Siding with the Allies in World War I, Japan extended its influence into former German colonies on mainland Asia, such as Shantung. Japan's economic growth continued, too: between 1910 and 1930 its production of metals, machinery, and textiles grew fourfold, and gas and electricity a staggering twenty-fourfold. The growth in overseas trade was also impressive.

In Japanese politics, however, all was not well. So-called "patriotic societies," like the Japanese National Essence Society (Dai Nihon Kokusuikai, founded 1919), called for a return to more conservative, patriotic ways. At the same time, politicians were finding it increasingly difficult to control the army. Groups of right-wing officers, such as the Cherry Blossom Society (Sakura-kai, founded 1930), said it was Japan's duty to protect Asia from evil Western influence. They also praised military glory, which they believed would flow from action against their oldest enemy, China.

Japanese soldiers are cheered as they leave for service on the Asian mainland. Scenes like this reflected the popular nationalism that emerged in interwar Japan.

The unattached giant

On the other side of the Pacific, the United States had undergone an even more spectacular change. After the close of the terrible Civil War (1861–65), it entered an extraordinary "gilded age" of industrialization and economic expansion. Between 1850 and 1900 the population rose from 23.2 million

FACT FILE

Boom America, 1921-29

● Average real incomes rose by 37 percent to $710 per annum.
● Industrial production rose 90 percent.
● By 1930 the United States was using over half the world's energy.

However, these figures hid real differences. Agricultural production and profits fell; older industries, such as coal, cotton, and shipbuilding stagnated; oil production and new automotive and electrical industries flourished.

to 76 million. In the 50 years before 1920, annual coal production soared from 22 million tons (20 million metric tons) to 625.5 million tons (568.6 million metric tons), oil output from 5.2 million barrels to 442.9 million barrels, and the value of exports from $451 million to $8.6 billion. Growth in banking, steel production, and engineering was equally remarkable. By the end of World War I the United States was indisputably the wealthiest nation on earth.

With money, industrial growth, and a large population came power. For a time before 1914 the United States joined other Western nations in taking over territories beyond its frontiers, such as the Hawaiian Islands and the Philippines. US imperialism, however, was small-scale by European standards. The United States was more interested in seeing that no other power threatened its commercial or security interests. The clearest example of this was its "open door" policy toward China.

VOICES

US imperialism

Hawaii is ours; Porto Rico is to be ours; at the prayer of her people Cuba finally will be ours; in the islands of the East, even to the gates of Asia, coaling stations are to be ours at the very least; the flag of a liberal government is to float over the Philippines …

US Senator Albert Beveridge, 1898

After its flirtation with imperialism and brief participation in World War I, the United States turned its back on further military escapades. It rejected the newly formed League of Nations, too, because it did not want to become entangled in European politics.

The Old World, so the popular feeling went, could only dirty the honesty and idealism of the New World. American needs, not some dream of world peace, should come first. During the 1920s, therefore, US administrations operated at arm's length from the rest of the world, concentrating on international treaties to maintain the peace and reduce armaments.

The Wall Street Crash of 1929 and the Great Depression that followed it reinforced America's inward-looking mood. The country had enough problems of its own, it was felt, to have to bother itself too much with the warlike antics of regimes thousands of miles away.

US-Japanese relations

During World War I, the United States had approved of vague claims by their Japanese allies to further territory on mainland Asia. By 1919, with the war over, the US government was beginning to wonder whether it had been wise to support such expansion: in the long run its policy would act against US interests in the Pacific. In November 1921, therefore, the United States called a conference in Washington, at which it was agreed that the size and firepower of all major British, US, and Japanese warships would be fixed at the ratio of 5:5:3. According to another agreement Britain, the United States, France, and Japan agreed to consult with each other if disputes arose in East Asia.

US-Japanese relations might have remained on an even keel if Japanese affairs had been left in the hands of men like Shidehara Kijuro, foreign minister 1924–27 and 1929–31. His desire was not for conquest but to further his country's prosperity. Others, including officers in the powerful Japanese army, had different views. By 1930 it was becoming increasingly clear that Britain and France, the old colonial powers in Asia, were in decline. A power vacuum was developing in the region and certain officers in Japan's Guangdong Army, based in the Korean border region, were eager to fill it.

VOICES

The United States goes her own way

The United States is the world's best hope, but if you fetter [chain] her in the interests and quarrels of other nations … you will destroy her power for good and endanger her very existence. Leave her to march freely through the centuries to come as in the years that have gone.

Senator Henry Cabot speaks for US independence in foreign affairs, 1919

Peace for the world? Watched by US Secretary of State Henry Stimson, Japanese ambassador Katsuji Debuchi signs the Kellogg-Briand Pact condemning war as a way of achieving a nation's aims, July 24, 1929.

When Japanese forces overran the Chinese province of Manchuria in 1931, President Herbert Hoover objected strongly and Secretary of State Stimson said the United States would not recognize any development in China brought about by force. Japan ignored them. Open confrontation with the United States was becoming more likely.

Japanese troops enter Manchuria in the wake of the so-called Mukden Incident, a suspicious sabotage attack on the Japanese-run South Manchuria Railroad.

FACT FILE

The Mukden Incident

On September 18, 1931, a section of Japanese-owned railroad near Mukden, in the northern Chinese province of Manchuria, was dynamited. Japanese forces, based in the area since 1905, responded by occupying all Manchuria and renaming it Manchukuo. By 1937 this puppet state accounted for 37 percent of Japan's iron production. It is now widely believed that the track sabotage was the work of the Japanese themselves.

4. THE MARCH TO WAR

The Great Depression made governments around the world deeply unpopular. Unemployed and often starving, the people of many nations turned to extremist parties with simple, stirring policies to lead them out of the slump. In Italy, Germany, and Japan, for instance, right-wing governments talked up their countries' virtues and promised foreign conquest. With the rest of the world focused on economic troubles, Japan invaded China as the first step to carving out an empire in Southeast Asia. The United States countered Japan's military aggression with economic warfare. This left the Japanese with a stark choice: back down, or prepare for war with the United States.

Japan's "semi-divine" supreme leader and figurehead, Emperor Hirohito, in military uniform, 1931.

FACT FILE

Military spending

Between 1920 and 1940, overall Japanese military spending increased from US$668 million to $3.1 billion. Spending on army equipment and aircraft rose swiftly from $12 million to $650 million. The spending increase on naval equipment and aircraft was less dramatic, rising from $82 million to $395 million. In comparison, US military spending fell from $3.3 billion in 1920 to $2.4 billion by 1940.

The neutral state

In the 1932 US presidential elections Franklin Delano Roosevelt beat President Hoover because the people believed Roosevelt would be better able to deal with the effects of the Great Depression.

Certainly this was the new president's main aim, but he was also much more concerned than Hoover about the rise of aggressive military powers around the world. The fascist Benito Mussolini already controlled Italy and from 1933 onward Hitler's Nazis were tightening their fearful grip on Germany.

Japan was not a fascist state and never became one, even during World War II. Nevertheless, its democratic system of government was not very deep rooted and all citizens owed their ultimate allegiance to the emperor, not the elected government. Moreover, the nonmilitary ministers found it very difficult to rein in hot-headed army officers, especially when so much of the army was based far away on the Asian mainland.

This lack of control had led to the capture of Manchuria, an event that had worried Roosevelt. Nevertheless, at this stage the people of the United States were unwilling to intervene actively to stop the spread of international aggression. Europe, they believed, should deal with its own problems, and the troubles in China, although serious, were too distant to worry the United States unduly.

The famous airman Charles Lindbergh, keen to keep the United States out of World War II, speaks at an "America First" rally in 1941.

VOICES

America First

I know I will be severely criticized by the interventionists in America when I say we should not enter a war unless we have a reasonable chance of winning …I do not believe that our American ideals, and our way of life, will gain through an unsuccessful war. And I know that the United States is not prepared to wage war in Europe successfully at this time.

Charles Lindbergh, 1940

America's peaceful mood was shown in 1935 when Congress passed the first Neutrality Act, banning US companies from supplying arms to any warring nation.

Although Roosevelt opposed the Act because it stopped the United States from helping nations that were being bullied, public support was so strong that he had no choice but to sign it into law. Two years later a poll showed that 94 percent of the US population still opposed any involvement in a foreign war. Over the months that followed, however, the mood began to change.

An epidemic of lawlessness

The Great Depression had hit Japan hard: between 1929 and 1931, for example, the value of its exports plummeted by nearly 50 percent. As in Germany, popular support for democracy fell because it was blamed for the country's woes; in contrast, more traditional, nationalist policies gained in popularity. In February 1936 a band of hot-headed young soldiers even assassinated leading politicians and seized part of central Tokyo in an attempt to overthrow the elected government. Although the coup failed, it

The coup that failed: Japanese troops of the Third Regiment trail through Tokyo on their way back to barracks after leaving the Metropolitan Police Department.

Shanghai under occupation, 1937. Japanese
troops march through the deserted streets
of the city they had taken after weeks of
ferocious fighting.

showed just how powerful and dangerous
the military had become.

Japan left the League of Nations in 1933.
Three years later it signed the Anti-
Comintern Pact with Nazi Germany, another
rogue state. The pact was an agreement to
resist all communism, especially that of the
Soviet Union. In 1938 and 1939 Japan
actually fought (and lost) two large battles
with the Soviets on the northern border of
Manchukuo (Manchuria) before signing a
neutrality pact with them in 1941. Shortly
after the agreement with the Nazis, Japan's
military commanders renewed the conquest
of China, following the Marco Polo Bridge
Incident of July 1937.

FACT FILE

Marco Polo Bridge Incident

A treaty of 1902 permitted Japan and
other nations to guard their interests in
China by stationing a few troops near
Beijing. By July 7, 1937, the Japanese force
had reached some 15,000 men, whose
aggressive nighttime training worried
the Chinese. When shots were fired near
the ancient granite Marco Polo Bridge at
Wanping, the skirmishing escalated to
full-scale fighting and within two weeks
Japan and China were at war.

By this time, Japanese aggression was beginning to gain a bad press in the United States. In October 1937 Roosevelt condemned "international lawlessness," a clear reference to Japan's behavior in China. Relations between the two countries grew even worse when, in December 1937, three bombers of the Imperial Japanese Navy sank the US gunboat *Panay* near Nanking. Three men were killed and 43 sailors and five civilians were wounded. The Japanese apologized, but it marked a new low in Japanese-US relations. The horrific treatment of Chinese civilians following the capture of Nanking alienated US opinion still further.

VOICES

President Roosevelt warns the world

The present reign of terror and international lawlessness began a few years ago. It began through unjustified interference in the internal affairs of other nations or the invasion of alien territory in violation of treaties; and has now reached a stage where the very foundations of civilization are seriously threatened.

October 5, 1937

Chinese farmers help wounded survivors from the USS *Panay* after Japanese bombers, mistaking its identity, had sunk it in the Yangtze River on December 12, 1937.

The path to Pearl Harbor

In order for Japan to be economically independent, especially in oil supplies, its government was determined to expand into Southeast Asia. By now it had the forces for such an operation: between 1936 and 1941 the size of Japan's army had doubled, while by 1940 the Imperial Japanese Navy was more powerful than both the US and British Pacific fleets combined. In September 1940 Japanese forces began moving into French Indochina (Vietnam, Cambodia, and Laos). The previous year the United States had canceled its ancient commercial treaty with Japan, leaving it free to cut trade. After the Japanese advance into Indochina, Roosevelt ordered economic sanctions against Japan. These denied it the raw materials, such as metals, that the anxious president believed Japan would need to continue its conquests.

The tactic failed. On July 25, 1941, Japanese troops moved unopposed into the rest of Indochina. Roosevelt's administration saw this as a clear threat to US interests in the Far East and on July 26 all Japanese assets in the United States were frozen. One week later, supported by the British and the Dutch, the United States banned the export of all oil to Japan.

Faced with the prospect of economic collapse and a withdrawal from the conquered territories, the Japanese military planned for war. By the middle of August they had agreed on a course of action. Japan would invade the Dutch East Indies in November, followed the next month by surprise attacks on British and US possessions in the Far East. The countdown to Pearl Harbor had begun.

Playing for time or last chance for peace? Japanese diplomat Saburo Kurusu speaks to suspicious-looking American reporters in Washington just a few days before his country attacked Pearl Harbor.

FACT FILE

The US Pacific Fleet

By the end of May 1941 the United States Pacific Fleet, with its headquarters at Pearl Harbor, Hawaii, consisted of nine battleships, three aircraft carriers, 12 heavy cruisers, eight light cruisers, 50 destroyers, and 33 submarines. These vessels were supported by carrier-based dive bombers, torpedo carriers and fighters as well as shore-based planes of the USAAF.

5. SUNDAY, DECEMBER 7, 1941

President Roosevelt condemned the surprise assault on Pearl Harbor as a "day which will live in infamy." In fact, there was nothing new or immoral about Japan's first strike. Catching the enemy unawares is a well-known military tactic. Moreover, although devastating, the Japanese plan was based on an out-of-date understanding of naval warfare. As the Battle of Pearl Harbor itself illustrated vividly, the future of war at sea rested with aircraft, carriers, and submarines, not battleships. Quite simply, Admiral Isoroku Yamamoto had chosen the wrong target.

Sitting ducks

Admiral Yamamoto had been planning the Pearl Harbor attack for almost a year, carefully studying the successful British air attack on the Italian Fleet in Taranto (November 1940). The purpose of Operation Z was to cripple the US Pacific Fleet, allowing Japanese forces to occupy all Southeast Asia unopposed. They could then move into the Indonesian Archipelago, a region rich in oil and rubber that Japanese imperialists called the "Southern Resource Area." Emperor Hirohito finally approved the plan on December 1, 1941. The Japanese embassy in Washington, DC, should have

delivered a declaration of war one hour before the attack began, but technical difficulties prevented this.

Five two-man midget submarines began the attack. Probably only one penetrated the harbor, firing a torpedo on target before it was sunk. The others were destroyed, abandoned, or simply disappeared. Although the United States had some success in this phase of the battle, there were serious shortcomings: The destroyer USS *Ward* sank an enemy submarine at 06:37, over an hour

Admiral Isoroku Yamamoto, commander-in-chief of the combined Japanese fleet 1941–43, whose careful planning was largely responsible for the success of the Pearl Harbor attack.

A unique Japanese photo of "Battleship Row" under attack. The plane that dropped the bomb can be seen peeling off to the right of the plume of water raised by its near miss.

before the first Japanese planes appeared, but the ship's reports did not trigger a general alarm.

Another lost opportunity came when a radar operator reported a huge flight of planes cluttering his screen. This was explained as a flight of B17 bombers due in from the mainland early that morning. What the operator had in fact spotted was a swarm of almost 180 Japanese Aichi D3A1 ("Val") dive bombers, Mitsubishi A6M2 ("Zero") fighters and Nakajima B5N ("Kate") bombers carrying torpedoes and conventional bombs.

Led by Commander Mitsuo Fuchida, they had taken off 90 minutes earlier and were now nearing the end of their 250-mile (440-kilometer) flight to Oahu. Below them, most people were enjoying a Sunday morning rest. Antiaircraft guns were unmanned, ammunition boxes locked, and ships lay still at their moorings. On the nearby airfields the planes were parked in neat rows, wingtip to wingtip—sitting ducks.

FACT FILE

The Nakajima B5N

Description:	Principal bomber used in Pearl Harbor attack
First flown:	1937
Name given by Allies:	"Kate"
Number built:	1,150 approx
Crew:	3 (pilot, commander, and rear gunner)
Max speed:	235 mph (378 km/h)
Range:	1,235 miles (1,992 km)
Armaments:	rear-facing machine gun; single 1,750-lb (800 kg) torpedo or bomb, or several smaller bombs

Pandemonium

The attack lasted barely 90 minutes and came in two waves, each made up of three groups of aircraft. At around 07:45 the slow and vulnerable torpedo bombers reached their target, skimming over the lagoon and dropping sleek missiles into the water before soaring away to rejoin the carriers out at sea.

Meanwhile, the fighters and other bombers were concentrating on the island's airfields Wheeler, Hickam, Kaneohe, and Bellows. Strafing and bombing, they destroyed 188 planes and damaged a further 159. Several of the incoming B17s arrived in the middle of the attack and, with insufficient fuel to get away, were among the casualties. A few US planes—some from a nearby carrier—managed to struggle into the air and join the handful of antiaircraft guns putting up some resistance. Five US planes were accidentally brought down by "friendly"

Utter devastation: the sunken minelayer *Ogala* lies in the foreground of this shot across Pearl Harbor, taken only an hour or so after the end of the Japanese attack.

FACT FILE

USS *Arizona*

Description:	Most dramatic casualty of Pearl Harbor attack
Launched:	1915
Displacement:	34,540 tons (31,400 metric tons)
Officers and crew:	1,385
Armaments:	12 x 14" guns, 12 x 5" guns, 12 x 5" antiaircraft guns
Armor:	hull: 8–14 in (200–360 mm); deck: 3 in (76 mm); turrets: 9–18 in (230–460 mm)
Fate:	Blew up and sank, with the loss of 1,177 crew, after a direct hit from a single bomb at 08:06

antiaircraft fire. During the entire operation the Japanese lost only 29 aircraft with 65 men killed or wounded.

The brunt of the assault fell on Pearl Harbor itself. Here, the principal targets were the proud mascots of the fleet: its eight mighty battleships. Within minutes, five were sunk or sinking and two damaged: USS *Arizona* exploded; USS *California*, the fleet flagship, was hit by torpedoes and bombs and went down; USS *West Virginia*, crippled by nine torpedoes, also sank; USS *Oklahoma* capsized after being holed by four torpedoes; USS *Nevada*, bombed, torpedoed, and on fire, was deliberately run aground; USS *Tennessee* was hit by two bombs and set alight by debris from the *Arizona*; only the USS *Maryland* escaped relatively unscathed. A further three cruisers, three destroyers, and a minelayer were also sunk or damaged.

By midday, having decided against a third wave of attacks, the Japanese fleet was preparing to leave the area before it was targeted by long-range US bombers. It left behind 2,402 Americans dead, 55 of them civilians killed by shells from their own antiaircraft guns, and some 1,200 wounded. Significantly, it also left intact oil supplies, shipyards, power stations, and the fleet's headquarters building. It was not worth wasting bombs on them, Yamamoto had argued: Once the US battleships and airforce were removed, the war would be as good as over.

The admiral was wrong. Far from ending the war, the attack on Pearl Harbor marked only its beginning.

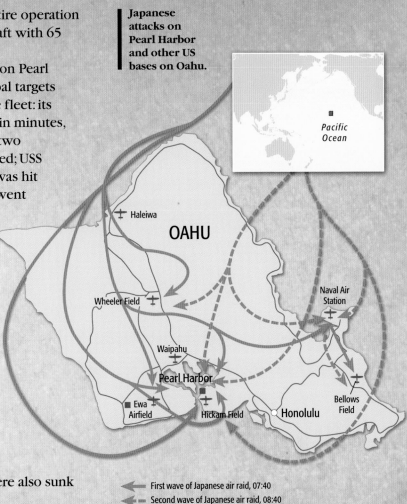

Japanese attacks on Pearl Harbor and other US bases on Oahu.

Pacific Ocean

OAHU

Haleiwa

Wheeler Field

Waipahu

Pearl Harbor

Ewa Airfield

Hickam Field

Honolulu

Naval Air Station

Bellows Field

First wave of Japanese air raid, 07:40
Second wave of Japanese air raid, 08:40
US airfield
US base

VOICES

Victory speech

Brilliant success was achieved for our country through the splendid efforts of you men. But we still have a great way to go. After this victory we must tighten the straps of our helmets and go onward, determined to continue our fight until the final goal has been won.

Admiral Nagumo to Pearl Harbor Attack Force, December 7, 1941

6. HOSTILITIES EXIST

The Battle of Pearl Harbor shocked the world. It came as a double blow to the United States. First, it showed the country to be less powerful and prepared than it had imagined. Second, although most Americans felt that war with Japan was likely, they believed that operations would begin much farther from home. America's friends and future allies were horrified, too.

VOICES

Churchill's despair

As I turned and twisted in bed the full horror of the news sank in upon me. There were no British or American capital ships in the Indian Ocean or the Pacific except American survivors of Pearl Harbor who were hastening back to California. Over this vast expanse of waters Japan was supreme and we were everywhere weak and naked.

British Prime Minister Winston Churchill reflects on the Allied position after the sinking of the *Repulse* and the *Prince of Wales* (see page 30).

Wearing a black armband as a symbol of mourning for those killed at Pearl Harbor, President Roosevelt signs the declaration of war against Japan, December 8, 1941.

Britain in particular had hoped that the mighty United States would soon enter the war and tip the balance against the German-Italian-Japanese Axis. The events of December 7, 1941, showed the United States to be less powerful than the British Prime Minister, Winston Churchill, had expected. Furthermore, US forces had taken a devastating hit. From an Allied point of view, therefore, the position at Christmas 1941 was grim indeed.

Declarations of war

The most obvious consequence of the sudden Japanese attack on US territory was the declaration of war. On December 8 President Roosevelt announced that, whether the United States willed it or not, "Hostilities exist" and "our people, our territory and our interests are in grave danger." Congress duly declared war on

Japan and the president signed the document. Three days later, in another somewhat surprising move, Germany and Italy declared war on the United States. Pearl Harbor had triggered what was now a genuinely worldwide war.

The Japanese lost no time in following up the victory at Pearl Harbor. Speed, they knew, was essential to make the maximum possible advances before the United States recovered itself sufficiently to consider a counterattack. Their aim was to sweep up the British and Dutch empire in Southeast Asia and protect their conquests with a string of Pacific island bases. The second part of this plan was just about complete by the end of the year, when Guam, Makin, and Wake, as well as the Marshall and Gilbert Islands, were all in Japanese hands. Apart from the main Hawaiian Islands, only Midway remained under US control.

The Japanese Empire at its greatest extent, 1942–43

Imperial conquest

Japan's attack on the Western colonial empires went equally well. It began with an assault on the Philippines which, although forewarned by the Pearl Harbor attack, were in precisely the same state of unpreparedness. Despite heroic resistance by General Douglas MacArthur, the Philippines were under Japanese control by late May 1942. Fearing a second attack on Hawaii, perhaps even an invasion, the US government decided not to meet MacArthur's repeated requests for reinforcements.

French Indochina (Vietnam, Cambodia, and Laos), partly occupied in 1940, had been under full Japanese control since July 1941. Soon after, Thailand became a Japanese ally. By March 1942 the Dutch East Indies (Indonesia and Borneo) were also within the swelling Japanese Empire. So too were the British possessions of Hong Kong, Malaya (including the prestigious port city of Singapore), and southern Burma.

Two British battleships sent as reinforcements to the area, HMS *Prince of Wales* and HMS *Repulse*, were sunk by Japanese dive bombers three days after the Pearl Harbor attack. Japan's next targets were New Guinea and Papua, thereby threatening Australia. Here the spectacular advance was finally thwarted.

Salvage and Doolittle

Once the Philippines had fallen, the base at Pearl Harbor became more important than ever for the US Pacific Fleet. It was now in the front line of defense and also had to serve as a springboard for counterattack.

FACT FILE

Fall of Singapore

On February 15, 1942, the British Army suffered one of its most humiliating defeats when the Japanese captured Singapore. This fortified city-state had recently been reinforced at great cost and was supposedly impregnable. Its big guns pointed toward the sea, however, and the defending garrison was inexperienced and poorly led. The attackers, although fewer in number, were battle-hardened, ferocious, and utterly ruthless.

One empire replaces another: delighted Japanese troops raise their Rising Sun flag over Singapore, which they took from the British in February 1942.

Death march: American soldiers and civilians captured on the Philippines are force-marched 60 miles (97 kilometers) from Bataan toward their prisoner-of-war camps. Nearly a quarter died of maltreatment and starvation en route.

According to traditional military thinking, large-scale offensives meant battleships, and enormous efforts were made to salvage the wrecks at Pearl Harbor and restore them to service. The *Arizona* was beyond repair, as was the *Oklahoma*, although it was raised. The five other badly damaged vessels were patched up and sent back to the mainland for complete refurbishment.

The battleships rejoined the fleet later in the war. However, the winner-takes-all gigantic fleet battle that Yamamoto had predicted never took place. By 1945 even the Japanese had come to see that the battleship was the dinosaur of the fleet—vast and impressive but on the verge of extinction.

FACT FILE

The Greater East Asia Co-Prosperity Sphere

To make his country's conquests sound less like an empire, Japanese Foreign Minister Matsuoka Yosuke announced, on August 1, 1940, the formation of the Greater East Asia Co-Prosperity Sphere. This was, he declared, a bloc of nations, led by Japan, that were free from any Western interference. In truth, the scheme's purpose was to serve the needs of the Japanese economy.

The Doolittle Raid, April 1942: a B-25 takes off from the USS *Hornet* to join Lieutenant Colonel Jimmy Doolittle's surprise bombing raid on Tokyo.

Meanwhile, the significance of what the December 7 raid had not achieved was becoming more apparent. A task force, comprising the aircraft carrier *Enterprise*, the cruisers *Northampton* and *Salt Lake City*, and six destroyers, all of which had been at sea at the time of the Pearl Harbor attack, was joined by the carrier *Hornet* and some other vessels to become Task Force 16. Having shelled enemy positions on occupied islands, Vice Admiral William F. Halsey led the force closer to Japan.

From deep within enemy waters, 16 twin-engined B-25 bombers were launched from the deck of the *Hornet* and, at noon on April 18, 1942, Tokyo experienced its first air-raid. Although the planes were shot down before they reached the safety of friendly Chinese airfields, the raid did wonders for US morale: the Japanese were not the only ones capable of launching surprise attacks from the air.

FACT FILE

Carrier battle

The Battle of the Coral Sea was the first fought between aircraft carriers. Both sides remained out of sight of each other. US losses included a carrier, a destroyer, and an oil supply vessel sunk, 69 aircraft destroyed, and 656 men killed. The Japanese lost a light carrier, a destroyer, and three small warships sunk, a large carrier and several other vessels severely damaged, 92 aircraft destroyed, and 966 men killed.

Equally significantly, the Doolittle Raid, as it was named, after the officer who planned and led it, showed that naval power was about more than just battleships.

Coral Sea

The same point was made even more powerfully two weeks later. Under the codename Operation MO, Japan planned to invade southern New Guinea and key positions in the neighboring Solomon

Islands. A large naval force under the command of Admiral Shigeyoshi Inoue was given the task of protecting the invasion fleet. US intelligence learned of the plan and Admiral Frank Fletcher led a combined US-Australian fleet to intercept the Japanese and, if possible, prevent the assault.

The Japanese invasion of Tulagi in the Solomons went ahead as planned, with only slight losses. The opposing forces, each featuring two large aircraft carriers, then entered the Coral Sea. Over May 7–8, 1942, they exchanged air strikes, each suffering considerable losses before they withdrew. As a consequence Admiral Inoue felt unable to guarantee cover for the New Guinea invasion and the operation was postponed for another day. That day never came.

The Battle of the Coral Sea saved Port Moresby, New Guinea's capital. It also put out of action two Japanese carriers that could have played a crucial role in the

fighting that lay ahead. Most significant of all, it showed that defeat at Pearl Harbor had neither hamstrung America's Pacific Fleet nor broken its will to wage war.

VOICES

The greatest battle

The greatest battle in the history of the US Pacific Fleet … was fought … in the Coral Sea … For five days, smudged with belching smoke screens and roaring with bomb bursts, a US naval force and army bombers from land bases took turns tearing into a heavy Jap task force, invasion-bound. For the Jap the going was too tough. His fleet was badly shot up.

Time Magazine May 18, 1942

Abandon ship! Men leap into the sea from the deck of the USS *Lexington* after it was fatally damaged by Japanese aircraft in the Battle of the Coral Sea, May 1942.

7 TOWARD HIROSHIMA

The Battle of the Coral Sea was the first indication that the Japanese advance across the Pacific toward the United States and Australia might be halted. This was confirmed at the Battle of Midway (June 1942). After this, the Pearl Harbor naval facilities played a vital role in the Allied drive for victory. The base remained the headquarters of the US Pacific Fleet and

FACT FILE

Admiral Nimitz

Chester W. Nimitz (1885–1966) was ultimately responsible for the Allied operations in the Pacific that destroyed the Japanese Empire after Pearl Harbor. One of World War II's most powerful men, he held a double command: commander-in-chief, United States Pacific Fleet, and commander-in-chief, all Allied air, land, and sea forces in Pacific Ocean Areas. His command was based in Pearl Harbor until January 1945, when he moved his headquarters to the island of Guam.

Despite the losses from the attack on Pearl Harbor, Admiral Nimitz managed to organize his forces to halt the Japanese advance.

was the station from where its remarkable commander-in-chief, Admiral Chester Nimitz, successfully guided operations. It was also where vital code-breaking work took place. Just as significant were the submarine operations from Pearl Harbor that sank millions of tons of enemy shipping, crippling Japan's ability to wage war.

Midway

The Japanese were slow to take advantage of their success at Pearl Harbor and it was not until the summer of 1942 that Admiral Yamamoto decided once again to threaten US control of the eastern Pacific. His target was not Oahu itself, which was considered too heavily defended, but the small atoll of Midway. Lying some 745 miles (1,200 kilometers) from Pearl Harbor at the northwest tip of the Hawaiian chain, it housed a US air and naval base but little else. Nevertheless it was of great strategic importance. Its capture would deprive US submarines of a key refueling point and make future direct attacks on Japan, like the Doolittle Raid, almost impossible.

Admiral Yamamoto's plan was to attack Midway with planes, then put troops ashore. When the remaining US Pacific Fleet carriers came to the rescue, he would blast them out of the water with planes and battleships. This would leave him in control of the eastern Pacific and perhaps persuade the United States to come to terms. It was not to be. During the ensuing battle US forces had the advantage of knowing the Japanese plans in advance, thanks to the code-breakers at Pearl Harbor. They also enjoyed several slices of good fortune.

When contact between the two sides was first made, the Japanese easily beat off attacks from outdated US aircraft and inflicted serious damage on the Midway base. They were taken totally unawares,

however, when 37 Douglas "Dauntless" dive bombers from the USS *Enterprise*, led to their target by following the wake of a Japanese destroyer, peeled into attack.

VOICES

Under attack

The terrifying scream of the dive-bombers reached me first, followed by the crashing explosion of a direct hit. There was a blinding flash and then a second explosion, much louder than the first. I was shaken by a weird blast of warm air …Then followed a startling quiet as the barking of guns suddenly ceased. I got up and looked at the sky. The enemy planes were already gone from sight.

Commander Mitsuo Fuchida remembers being under attack at Midway

Within minutes the undefended carriers *Kaga* and *Akagi*, their decks cluttered with aircraft being refueled and rearmed, were set ablaze. Soon USS *Yorktown's* bombers joined the assault and caused similar damage to the carrier *Soryu*. All three of the gigantic warships, the very heart of the imperial fleet, were eventually abandoned and scuttled. Yamamoto's 11 large Japanese battleships, positioned behind the carriers with the intention of finishing off the weakened Americans, never got into the fight.

The battle continued for another two days. By the end the Japanese had lost four carriers, two cruisers, three destroyers, some 270 aircraft, and around 3,500 men. US losses amounted to a single carrier, a destroyer, about 150 aircraft, and 307 men. Pearl Harbor and the Hawaiian chain of islands were secure and the task of taking the war to the Japanese could now begin.

FACT FILE

Station HYPO

Japan's Navy, Army and diplomatic service used different code systems to keep their messages secret. US and British experts broke the diplomatic code before the attack on Pearl Harbor. Code breakers at Pearl Harbor's Station HYPO broke enough of the Japanese Navy code, JN-25, in time to provide vital information on enemy plans before the Battle of Midway.

Rulers of the Pacific skies: US "Dauntless" dive bombers on patrol above Midway Island after a Japanese plan to seize the base had been foiled in June 1942.

US troops scramble ashore on Guadalcanal in the Solomon Islands as part of the Allies' gradual advance across the Pacific towards Japan.

Island hopping

There were three strategies open to Admiral Nimitz. He could direct the main thrust of his attack on Japan from the southeast, perhaps using bases in China; the northern route via the Aleutian Islands was another option; the third possibility was the direct route, "island hopping" across the Pacific directly toward Japan itself. It was that strategy which the admiral chose, believing it gave him the best chance of bringing Japan within range of his heavy bombers. Bombing, he predicted correctly, would finally bring the enemy to its knees.

Pearl Harbor remained the headquarters of US operations until 1945. It was from here that Nimitz masterminded the campaigns around the Solomon Islands in 1942–43 and the drive across New Guinea in 1944. Meanwhile, US air, sea, and land forces were retaking the Gilbert Islands, the Marshall Islands, and the Marianas. Okinawa, the large island to the south of Japan, was captured after a horrific battle that lasted from March until June 1945. By the summer of 1944 long-range US bombers had been pounding Japanese cities with frightful regularity.

FACT FILE

Subs at Pearl Harbor

By 1944 the US submarine base at Pearl Harbor employed more than 6,500 personnel. Hundreds of submarines were serviced there, enabling them to make 499 patrols across the Pacific. Their mission to seek out and destroy enemy warships and merchant ships was remarkably successful: The Pearl Harbor patrols sank shipping amounting to 2,210,718 tons (2,009,744 metric tons).

VOICES

Little warning of attack

It was a trying period, as little, if any, warning was being given by the radars in the Force, and at times the first indication of an aircraft approaching was visual sighting by the close screen. The picket destroyers were invaluable with their visual sightings. The CAP [Combat Air Patrol] shot down a total of 12 aircraft and Task Force antiaircraft fire splashed [shot down into the sea] 21 more.

From an official US report on the attack on the island of Kyushu, March 1945

The US Pacific Fleet was now a truly awesome fighting force. America's huge industrial capacity had built it up into something far larger and more powerful than anything even imagined by any prewar power. At its heart lay not the battleships that Yamamoto had sought to destroy in his December 7 attack back in 1941, but dozens of gigantic aircraft carriers. Seventeen of these were of the huge Essex Class, each 38,280 tons (34,800 metric tons), 869 feet (265 meters) long, 147 feet (44.95 meters) wide, and capable of handling 90 large aircraft. Bristling with antiaircraft weaponry and able to remain at sea for weeks without refueling, they were little short of floating airfields.

The end, when it came, was in a form even more nightmarish than anything the mighty Pacific Fleet could deliver. By 1945 it was clear that there was no way the Japanese could win the war. Surrender, however, was alien to their culture, an unthinkable disgrace. This explained the kamikaze attacks—the deliberate and suicidal crashing of aircraft into US ships. It also explained why 20,700 men died defending Iwo Jima while only 216 handed themselves in as prisoners. At this point President Harry S. Truman, who had succeeded President Roosevelt in April 1945, had a fateful decision to make. He could order the invasion of Japan, which might well cost an estimated one million US lives, or he could use his country's deadly new secret weapon, the atomic bomb.

Truman chose the bomb. On August 6, 1945, the Japanese city of Hiroshima was obliterated in the world's first nuclear attack. Three days later, Nagasaki suffered the same unspeakable fate. On August 15, after bitter discussions among government ministers, Emperor Hirohito gave permission for his country to surrender. After three years, eight months, and nine days of bloodshed, the bitter harvest sown at Pearl Harbor had finally been gathered in.

Smoke pours from the stricken USS *Ticonderoga* after it has come under attack from Japanese kamikaze planes.

The ultimate revenge for Pearl Harbor? A gigantic mushroom cloud looms over the obliterated Japanese city of Nagasaki after the United States' second nuclear attack, on August 9, 1945. Japan surrendered six days later.

8 ONGOING ALERT

Pearl Harbor remains the base port of the US Pacific Fleet, the world's largest naval unit. It also houses a visitor center that each year attracts thousands of tourists eager to learn more about the harbor's place in history. The very phrase "Pearl Harbor" has entered the vocabulary of US culture. Today it is used to mean not simply the port and dockyards but the attack of December 7, 1941.

VOICES

Cold, hard interests

We will continue to be a Pacific power …because we have cold, hard interests in a region that accounts for half the world's people, much of its resources, a quarter of its goods and services, and most of its biggest militaries. Our security and prosperity depend on our engagement where the interests of so many powers converge, and where we fought three wars in the last half-century.

Anthony Lake, assistant to US president Bill Clinton, 1996

The devastating terrorist assault on New York City, that occurred on September 11, 2001, reminded many Americans of the surprise attack on Pearl Harbor, 60 years previously.

"Remember Pearl Harbor," the watchword for remaining alert and on guard, guided US thinking throughout the long period of the Cold War (1946–90) that followed World War II. Never again, the military promised, would the United States be caught unawares. However, when the communist threat dwindled away, vigilance declined too. Ten years later the United States faced its second "Pearl Harbor": the surprise attacks on New York's World Trade Center and the Pentagon on September 11, 2001.

Constant watchfulness

Shortly after the surrender of Japan and the end of World War II, the United States became involved in the Cold War. This was a struggle for world domination between communist countries, led by the Soviet Union (Russia), and capitalist-democratic countries, led by the United States. Although there was no direct fighting between the two superpowers, there were local conflicts in which they backed opposing sides. Some of the larger conflicts took place in Korea, Vietnam, and the Middle East.

At the same time there was always the possibility that one of the superpowers might try to knock the other out with an unannounced Pearl-Harbor-type strike. This would have been so much more devastating than the 1941 raid because after 1949 both sides had nuclear weapons. An attack with atomic or hydrogen bombs, delivered by giant, high-flying bombers or supersonic intercontinental missiles, would not just sink battleships but wipe out entire cities and threaten life across the whole planet.

VOICES

The Iron Curtain

From Stettin in the Baltic to Trieste in the Adriatic an iron curtain has descended across the Continent. Behind that line lie all the capitals of the ancient states of Central and Eastern Europe ... all these famous cities ... lie in ... the Soviet sphere, and all are subject ... to Soviet influence [and] to a very high and, in many cases, increasing measure of control from Moscow.

Winston Churchill's speech of March 5, 1946, that is said to have marked the start of the Cold War

Never again? This early warning station, based on Canadian soil, is part of a network intended to ensure that no enemy attack will ever again catch the United States unawares.

Each superpower set up elaborate detection systems to avoid being taken by surprise: This time there would be no repeat of the Pearl Harbor radar operator's unheeded warning. Huge radar dishes scanned the skies every minute of every day. Airborne Early Warning and Control planes (AWACs) and spy planes kept a constant watch from above the clouds; spies fed back information on enemy plans and installations; and in the 1980s the United States worked on a highly sophisticated "Star Wars" antimissile shield. Fortunately for the human race, these systems were never tested for real.

The nearest they came was in 1962 when the Soviets were discovered to be building and equipping missile launch sites on Cuba.

The sites were eventually dismantled and the weapons withdrawn, but for a few horrifying days it looked to the watching world as if the fingers poised above the nuclear launch buttons might actually descend.

FACT FILE

The Cuban Missile Crisis

In 1962 President John F. Kennedy learned that the Soviet Union had installed a nuclear missile base on the Caribbean island of Cuba. He ordered the US Navy to blockade the island. When Soviet ships carrying missiles approached, it looked as if the two superpowers might go to war. Fortunately the Soviet ships turned back, the United States agreed not to invade Cuba, and Armageddon was avoided.

President John F. Kennedy faces the press during the Cuban Missile Crisis of October 1962.

Yesterday and today: this aerial shot of modern Pearl Harbor shows a warship being made ready for sea and, in the mid-right of the picture, the concrete memorial marking the place where the USS *Arizona* was sunk in 1941.

The base today

Centered on Pearl Harbor, the US Pacific Fleet patrols 100 million square miles (260 million square kilometers), more than half the Earth's surface, and stretching from the west coast of the Americas right across the Pacific and Indian Oceans to the eastern shore of Africa. To cover such a vast area, it has 180 ships and 1,500 aircraft and employs 125,000 sailors, marines, and civilians. In recent years it has played a major role in US operations in the Persian Gulf.

In 1964 the US government declared Pearl Harbor to be a National Historic Landmark. Tourist activities are based on the USS Arizona Visitor Center, which attracts around 1.5 million visitors a year. The actual USS *Arizona* Memorial is a large concrete structure built above the place where the battleship sank on December 7, 1941.

Pearl Harbor is also the final resting place of another huge battleship. This is the USS *Missouri*, the US warship on which, on September 2, 1945, the formal surrender of Japan was signed before representatives of the victorious Allied powers. So, in the calm blue-green waters of Pearl Harbor, the warship whose sinking marked the start of the Pacific War and the vessel that witnessed the final end of that dreadful conflict lie side by side.

GLOSSARY

administration Government.

allegiance Sworn loyalty to a person or state.

Allies The countries, including Britain, France, and the United States, that fought together during World War I and World War II.

Armageddon The mythical end of the world.

ambassador A diplomatic official of the highest rank, sent by one country to another as its representative.

atoll A ring-shaped coral reef and small island, enclosing a lagoon and surrounded by open sea.

barracks Military accommodations.

blockade Prevent trade by cutting off all sea and land movement.

civilian An ordinary civilian, as opposed to a member of the armed forces

Cold War The period of high tension between the United States and the Soviet Union, lasting from 1946 to 1990.

colony A territory owned by a state beyond its borders.

communism Belief in a system in which capitalism is overthrown and the state controls wealth and property.

coup A change of government by force.

decommissioned Withdrawn from service.

dive bomber A plane that bombs its target while diving steeply toward it.

dredge Deepen a waterway.

dry dock A dock from which the water can be pumped, making it possible to work on a ship's hull.

embargo A ban on trade with a particular country.

fascism A nationalistic, often racist, ideology that favors strong leadership and does not tolerate dissent.

fetter Confine, restrict, or restrain.

Great Depression The major downturn in the world economy that lasted from 1929 to 1939 and resulted in high unemployment and widespread poverty.

imperialism The policy of taking over and governing territories beyond one's own national borders.

intelligence Information about secret plans or activities, especially those of enemies.

kamikaze A suicide mission carried out by a World War II Japanese pilot. He would fly his aircraft, packed with explosives, into an enemy target, often a ship.

League of Nations The international organization for peace and cooperation that operated between 1919 and 1946.

Manchuria A province of northeastern China.

midget submarine A two-man submarine launched from a larger submarine.

"open door" policy A policy of making sure that trade with a certain state (especially China) was open to everyone.

power vacuum When a major power (normally a state or empire) collapses and no other power rises immediately to take its place.

sabotage Deliberate damage, usually to machinery or transportation.

sanctions Measures taken by one or more nations to exert pressure on another nation to abide by international law.

Soviet Union Officially known as the Union of Soviet Socialist Republics (USSR), a communist-ruled federation of 15 republics, dominated by Russia, that lasted from 1922 to 1991.

strafe Attack from the air with machine-gun fire.

FURTHER INFORMATION

BOOKS

Air Raid—Pearl Harbor! The Story of December 7, 1941 by Theodore Taylor (Houghton Mifflin Harcourt, 2001)

The Attack on Pearl Harbor: the United States Enters World War II by John C. Davenport (Chelsea House, 2008)

A Boy at War: A Novel of Pearl Harbor by Harry Mazer (Simon & Schuster, 2001)

Days that Shook the World: Pearl Harbor by Paul Dowswell (Wayland, 2004)

History Firsthand: Pearl Harbor by Don Nardo (Greenhaven Press, 2001)

Pearl Harbor by Judy L. Hasday (Chelsea House, 2000)

Turning Points in History: Pearl Harbor by Richard Tames (Heinemann, 2001)

WEBSITES

www.eyewitnesstohistory.com/himpearlharbor2.htm
A Japanese film taken from the planes as they attacked Pearl Harbor.

www.eyewitnesstohistory.com/pearl.htm
An excellent personal account from a survivor of the USS *Arizona*.

www.iwm.org.uk/upload/package/25/pearl_harbour/index.htm
The British Imperial War Museum's thorough and objective account of the battle.

plasma.nationalgeographic.com/pearlharbor
A National Geographic multimedia presentation on the battle.

www.nps.gov/valr/index.htm
A guide to the US "Valor in the Pacific" national monument.

INDEX

Page numbers in **bold** refer to pictures.